- 3
- HOLE
- PRESS

Performances from this book for non-commercial
personal or educational purposes are encouraged,
provided the Author and Publisher are acknowledged.

For associated rights, permissions inquiries,
and other media rights, please contact 3 Hole Press.

For all professional and production rights,
please contact the Author.

First Edition
ISBN: 978-0-9982763-2-8

Printed in the USA on recycled paper.
Distributed by Small Press Distribution
Design by Omnivore

3 Hole Press gratefully acknowledges support from
the Brooklyn Arts Council and the New York State
Council on the Arts Literature Program.

3 Hole Press
Brooklyn NY
3holepress.org

WHEELCHAIR

A Play by
Will Arbery

Introduction
by Bill Callahan

plays represent possibility. like the knock on the door

just past the top of the opening of this one, when devon arrives, it's a loud rap or a timid tap—jarring and annoying even. or so quiet you aren't sure you heard it maybe, but full of possibility any way it's delivered. watching a movie or reading a novel there are moments when you might say 'that would never happen,' but you don't say it during a play—anything can happen because it's actually happening! a play isn't about who we were or what we might become. a play is about what we are right now at this moment because a play is as alive as its audience.

wheelchair made me think: we don't talk about sex enough. we don't talk about dreams at all. we go along pushing our dreams aside as nonsense, and trying to push the sex aside as nonsense but they are cleaved to everything that we are. it feels like we only talk about a few things these days. with all the chatter there is. but we aren't talking about the primal things that we need to establish first before we can move on. we're living without addressing those things that would open up the door to insight into the things we are talking (poorly) about.

everything is talking in this play. the refrigerator, the chair— and i never once thought, 'that would never happen.' they are talking towards that primal place. there is promise and destruction and nurturing and revulsion and old stews left on the stove and clean bowls and empty bellies and people leaving because they need a second. all of these people (and appliances) need a second. they need a second to think.

we all need a second to think. we really do.

—BC
    13 dec 2017

Will Arbery <warbery@gmail.com>

to Matthew ▾

8/11/16 ☆

Hi Matthew,

I hope all is well with you and that your trip out to California was wonderful. I'm writing because my proposal to Dixon Place was accepted, and they'd like me to present my piece on **Monday, December 19th** at **7:30 PM**. Are you available that night, and would you be willing to perform in my piece? We'd rehearse on weekends to accommodate your schedule. Also, I checked in with the theater, and they assure me that it's ADA accessible.

As I mentioned before, the show is about a man living alone (that's you). He is on stage periodically, and in the meantime, his furniture talks to each other. Then, the man's niece shows up and brings him some disturbing news from the outside world. It will run about an hour, and will be very manageable to memorize, rehearse, and stage. I'm still working on the script, but I'll send it to you as soon as I have it. I'm actually thinking that the character will be Gordon Sanders, an extenuation of your character in Your Resources!

I'm really excited about the possibility of making this show with you, and I hope we can make this work! Let me know. Talk soon.

...

Matthew S. Joffe

to me ▾

8/11/16 ☆

Hi Will:

In a word, YES! I am thrilled. Yes, plan a meeting/time to talk. Great news for a humid day.

Many thanks.

Matthew

Will Arbery <warbery@gmail.com>   11/23/16 ☆

to bcc: Olivia, bcc: Tomas, bcc: WEI-YI, bcc: Thomas, bcc: John, bcc: Sarah, bcc: Tressa, bcc: Hayward, bcc: Alexander, bcc: Maki, bcc: Casey, bcc: Casey, bcc: Natal ▼

friends,

writing to invite you to a show on the horizon. it would mean so much to me if you could make it to the workshop production of a new play of mine on **december 19** at dixon place. it's called WHEELCHAIR, and i developed it specifically for a wonderful performer named matthew joffe. this is a scary & strange little piece about change, disability, and evacuation. it would be mean a lot to have you there to experience it in its first go-round.

it's a little over an hour. and if adjectives ever convince you to go to things -- it's funny and weird and sad. i hope! the cast and team are absurdly talented and also across-the-board wonderful people. the piece is about being forced to change. to leave a room that you'd gotten used to.

anyhow -- really hope you can make it. hope you're having a peaceful week.

will

more info:

WHEELCHAIR
by Will Arbery
Directed by Will Arbery & Jacob Brandt
December 19ᵗʰ – 7:30PM
Dixon Place
161A Chrystie Street

Gordon lives alone with a severe disability. Even though he believes himself to be one of 36 righteous people in the world, Gordon is being evicted from his apartment by his niece. Meanwhile, his apartment is convulsing into the strange slow puppetry of loss. This is a strange and funny new play about being one of the righteous, about being forced to change, about furniture that talks, and about feeling broken.

Info HERE // Tickets HERE

Featuring Matthew Joffe, Alexander Paris, Rachel Sachnoff, Dan Giles, Mara Nelson-Greenberg, Jacob Brandt, and Jack Plowe

Design by Kimie Nishikawa and Daniel Prosky

Produced by Sam Barickman

Dramaturgy by Kate Kremer

Photos courtesy of Dixon Place

Wheelchair

Characters

GORDON 60s, Jewish. Uses a walker because of severe spinal problems.

DEVON 19, black

SASCHA 26, Jewish

CHAIR broken

FAN oscillating

CARD TABLE ashamed

FRIDGE dying

Setting

Gordon's apartment. A Hasidim/hipster block in West Williamsburg, Brooklyn.

Note

On casting and ability

This play was created for its brilliant original
performers: Rachel Sachnoff, Alexander Paris,
and Matthew Joffe. Matthew is a performer/
educator/activist, who has an extremely rare
craniofacial disorder called Moebius Syndrome.
Not everyone who plays Gordon needs to have
this exact disorder. But no one who plays Gordon
should be "acting" a disability he doesn't have.
Depending on who is cast, we can work together
to change certain lines accordingly.

On sound

This play works best with an ominous hum
underneath everything, almost imperceptible, but
enough to get in our brains. The play also works
best if everyone is wearing a microphone. We
initially came up with this for practical needs of
the performers. But it's great. Because then they
can whisper. Sascha's monologue can find itself in
a foggy terror. Devon can go on wild near-mut-
tered tangents. Gordon can whisper out his final
goodbye to his apartment. Everything becomes
just slightly stranger.

On puppetry

The fan can oscillate. The fridge's light can burst
back on. Other than that, the puppetry should be
minimal. The goal should not be cuteness.

Gordon's small & dirty apartment.

The rooms are: kitchen, living room, bedroom, bathroom.

In the kitchen: a mini-fridge, a dead toaster-oven.

In the living room: a record player, a card table, an uncomfortable chair.

In the bathroom: a toilet, a stack of newspapers.

In the bedroom: an air mattress on an army cot, an oscillating fan.

We hear the sound of construction—maybe a couple floors down—drilling, hammering, sawing, whirring, and maybe a construction worker being like: "That guy's a fucking retard, he's a fucking retard," just like the construction worker outside my building right now.

Anyway, Gordon walks on stage. He uses a wheeled walker to walk. He comes into the living room, sits down.

He eats fast food out of the bag, chewing slowly. It takes as long as it takes.

Then he goes over to the record player and puts on a Barbra Streisand record. "Where is the Wonder" from *My Name Is Barbra*.

He sits back down and reads the newspaper.

GORDON
Wow
Look at these
Look at this niceness here
Wow, these
Look at this niceness these people have here
Oh wow
Oh

As he walks into his bedroom, he says:

I love Barbra. I love her. What can I say?
I love her.
I love her so much. I love her so much.
I love her.

When he's gone, a piece of furniture might
start singing along to the song. It's okay if we
don't register this.

In his room, Gordon changes his shirt. He
takes off the shirt that he's wearing, slowly,
and then starts putting on the other shirt.
And this can take as long as it needs to take.

Barbra Streisand is still playing on the
record player.

Gordon brings the fan out into the kitchen,
plugs it in, turns it on.

He goes to the fridge, gets out some hors
d'oeuvres. Some cheese, some olives, some
crackers. He puts them on the card table.
He gets a bottle of wine, and he puts that on
the table too.

The record stops playing.

> Gordon sits down in the chair and talks to himself.

I went to that uh
Little market today.
So expensive but
They really do have
The most amazing

> Long pause.

It's getting

> Long pause.

I almost fell.

> Long pause.

And then I think
I really think that someone hit me on the
back of the head.
I don't know why they would
It felt that way.
It's not so
There's still good things.
I should have
I'm an idiot!

> Then there's a knock at the door.

> And now Devon is in the living room.

GORDON
Oh, hello!
Hello, I'm Gordon.

DEVON
Hey. I'm Devon.

GORDON
Great, Devon. I'm Gordon.
Thank you for coming.

DEVON
Yeah of course. Thank *you*.
It's nice to finally meet you

GORDON
You too

DEVON
It's good to put a face to the

GORDON
Yes, a face. And a
Well
Well, this is where I live. Come in.

DEVON
Great.

GORDON
Would you like to sit down in this chair?

DEVON
Sure.

                    Devon sits down.

Wait, what about you?

GORDON
What about me?

DEVON
Is there another chair?

GORDON
Oh, no, but look!

> He sits down on his walker, which doubles
> as a chair.

DEVON
Oh great.

GORDON
It's more comfortable than that chair anyway.

DEVON
Yeah this chair is uh
Haha

> Pause.

GORDON
Would you like some hors d'oeuvres?

DEVON
Um, sure.

GORDON
Great, yes, I have all of this.
All of this, so make yourself at
Eat as much as you want.

> Devon takes a little and eats.

DEVON
Is that wine?

GORDON
Yes, that is. Would you like some?

DEVON
Yeah.

GORDON
Are you old enough?

DEVON
No, actually.

> Gordon laughs and then pours the wine
> for Devon.

Thanks.

> Devon drinks all of the wine in his glass, and
> then pours himself another glass.

GORDON
Can we
Um
How does that feel?

DEVON
The wine?

GORDON
Yes.

DEVON
Good, I love wine. Thanks sorry, I had the
craziest day, so when I saw the wine, I was just

GORDON
Yes it's
Can we

Pause.

DEVON
What

Pause.

GORDON
What was crazy about your day?

DEVON
Well, I'm between apartments so I just
And I had a revelation that like made me sob

GORDON
What was the revelation?

DEVON
Oh nothing
I'm just scared
I've just been so scared recently
And I found another thing to be scared about

GORDON
Don't be scared
Everything is gonna be

Pause.

Should we look around the place? At what I have?

DEVON
Sure. Yeah. And thank you again.

They walk to the kitchen.

GORDON
So, this is
All this

DEVON
I can have any of this?

GORDON
You can have any of this

DEVON
This record player is nice.

GORDON
Yes, I ordered that!
From Target.com.

They walk to the bedroom.

DEVON
Is that an air mattress?

GORDON
Yes, it is.

DEVON
You're like poorer than I am.

GORDON
Oh. Thanks.
I used to have more money, but then
Well, I'll just say it:
I'm a lamed-vavnik.

DEVON
What?

GORDON

I'm one of only 36 righteous people in
the world. I'm very important but very
humble. I live a very humble life, and I'm an
exemplar of avanah. Which is humility.

DEVON

Oh.

GORDON

Yes.
I'm Jewish

DEVON

Cool

GORDON

What are you?

DEVON

Nothing
Jehovah's Witness
But I'm not
A witness

GORDON

Wow! Wow!
Jehovah's Witness wow
Fascinating the way they...yes
Yes, it's important to be a witness
It's important to surrender
Yes, there's very little choice
There's very little that we can control
Yes, all of our choices are very small,
and the rest is
Well we just don't know.
We just never know what will happen.
All we can do is what we do.

And then it all goes wrong anyway.
And then it all ends anyway.
And well there's just nothing we can do.

DEVON
Oh yeah.

GORDON
Great, great. So much in common.
Thank you for talking to me so much on the
internet, even when the conversation moved
past furniture.

DEVON
Oh, yeah. Thank you for giving me all your
furniture for free.

GORDON
It was the least I could do.
You made me feel so
It was just very exciting to talk to you.

DEVON
Yeah, you too.

GORDON
It was just very exciting to talk sexual.
I love words, and the sexual things that
they can do.

DEVON
Right?

GORDON
Right.
I didn't say everything I wanted to say,
because I was in a public library.
I don't have a computer here.

DEVON
Oh, yeah haha sometimes I was like...
on the train.
And I'd be like, hiding my phone, like *ahh
nobody look, I'm being erotic.*
And uhh I read this blog about the relationship
between language and hypnosis and sex and so
I was using some of those tips from that.

GORDON
Oh, well you did a good job.

DEVON
Thanks.
What else did you want to say?

GORDON
When?

DEVON
On the computer at the library

GORDON
I don't know, the moment has passed.

> Pause.

What I want to say now is
You're very...

DEVON
What, I'm very what?

GORDON
Well you're very beautiful.
Haha
And how young are you?

DEVON
Thanks
Uh thanks yeah and
I'm 19.

GORDON
Great. Okay.

DEVON
Why?

GORDON
No I don't know.

        Pause.

No.

        Pause.

Haha sorry.
It's okay. Sorry.

DEVON
Okay.
Well it was really cool to meet you
I'm glad we made such a cool arrangement
It was really a lifesaver and, so, should I
take the stuff now?

GORDON
Sure. Wait.
I don't know.
I'm having second thoughts.

DEVON
About what?

GORDON
Leaving.
I'm so sad.

DEVON
Oh, fuck. I'm sorry.
Why are you leaving?

GORDON
My niece is making me.
She's got a lot of attitude.
I have nothing good going for me, except my
righteousness.

DEVON
Well it sounds like your righteousness is like
Extra great.

GORDON
Thanks. It's what I have I guess.

DEVON
It's cool that you're so humble because
I'm all-powerful?

> Gordon laughs.

GORDON
You're all-powerful?

DEVON
Yes.

> Gordon laughs harder. The construction
> noises get louder. The lights flicker.

What is that?

GORDON

It must be the construction
They're tearing this place apart
Tell me more about how you're all-powerful
Hahaha!

DEVON

Don't laugh at me. I'll punch you if you keep
laughing at me. Whoops. Sorry, I didn't mean
to say that, it's just a trigger. No I have to say
this: I own the world! I just allow you to live
in it! No, that's not what I meant, listen. I don't
just say that because, like, I think it's *true*.
I don't think it's true. No, it is true! It's like, it's
like. No, listen. It's like. Okay. We *all* own the
world. And like. We *all* just allow each *other* to
live in *our* worlds. It's like, have you ever heard
the thing about how we're just simulations in
a video game? I think that's true except I think
the users are all of us, like we're all living
simulations, the control of which are crowd-
sourced to millions and millions of people,
and the goal is to try to figure out what to do
with this life. It's like, we're all really selfish,
and you just hide how selfish you are by being
really "nice" to "people" all the "time." There
are all kinds of people in the world. There's like
pretty people and other people. There's loud
people and quiet kids. Like, the indoor kids.
Like, the deep cuts. And then there's me. I've
figured everything out and I'm waiting till
I'm officially considered an adult so that I can
finally just go be awesome. That's why I moved
to NYC in a manner akin to Patti Smith and
that's why I'm figuring out how to get a bunch
of furniture for free, and then I'll conquer the
world. I know everyone here thinks that I need

Wheelchair

to get knocked down a couple pegs, but I
already *have* been knocked down a couple pegs,
like on *purpose*, like on my own, I knocked
my*self* down, because I *GET* it, I really get it,
but like, if I was really my full self, I would
be like, ten thousand pegs higher. Okay, listen.
I don't have any siblings. So sometimes when I
was a kid I would just walk around in my back
yard. And I would take my stuffed animals
with me. And I would talk to them, and I
would tell them things. My mom called them
my affirmations. Like I'd do these affirmations
for my toys. And it was like "you're gonna be
the best bear in the whole world, you're gonna
be the biggest and the meanest and the
smartest and the bravest and the best. All the
bears are going to love you. All the bears
already do." And like "you're the prettiest Jar
Jar Binks in the whole world. You're the queen
of the Jar Jar Binks. There's not one single other
Jar Jar Binks as great as you. It's a Jar Jar Binks
world and you're *the* Jar Jar Binks guy." And
this is going to sound so crazy but eventually
they started talking back, they were like…
"you're really cool, too." And I was like "no,
I'm not, I'm just a skinny little kid who talks to
his toys." And they were like, "no you're not.
We're inside the game. One day it's not going to
be cool to talk to us so you need to remember
what we say." And they told me everything.
In my backyard. And I listened. Well, it's like…
I don't know, it's like. I don't know. I don't know.
I don't know. I don't know. I mean I don't know.
I don't know. I don't know. I mean I don't know.
I don't know. Well I'm scared to be myself
because everyone puts me down for it? And I'm
hung up on a guy. We started as fuck buddies.

For a year and a half. Moved in together
because we were both desperate for a place.
And fell in love with each other. But now, I feel
even more lonely than before. I can't talk to
him, he barely touches me. And yet he doesn't
want me to be with anyone else. Yeah. But
meanwhile there is someone else who wants to
hold me and calls me beautiful every time we
talk. And I can't be with that person.

GORDON
Me?

DEVON
Oh, no. Sorry.
What am I doing? I hate talking. Everyone
always cuts me off mid sentence or replies with
"Oh." or "Yeah." and I hate it, damn it. I'm
scared to go outside. I'm scared all the angry
old people can see how free I am. I auditioned
for a show and I didn't get it and I've never
felt lower. I was perfect for it. I just wish they
would tell me why I didn't get it. I can't help
but feel trapped. I'm depressed, and I can't just
stop. I want to stop but I can't just *stop*. If I
did I would destroy the few I still love. I can't
even do drugs, and can't do anything right.
I lay on the ground silently screaming trapped
in my mind watching this body live on as
I desperately hope it dies. But actually I'm
really optimistic. I'm just looking for what is
good in this world. There are some people,
like me, who want what is good for the world.
And those who want the good, we are the good
in this world. Our love, and our hope. Fresh
fruit and vegetables are good. Lots of water is
good. Friends are good. Revolution is good.
Why am I still talking. Okay, okay.

Wheelchair

GORDON
Wow, here's what's so funny!
If we're all "simulations," like you say
Or if we're all "given to ourselves by God,"
like I say
Then how can we do such crazy things like
talk so long about nothing? Like you just did?
That feels like an error
What you just did felt like an error
Devon do you ever feel real?

DEVON
What
Yeah
Kind of
Do you

GORDON
Kind of
I'm losing my bearings

DEVON
It's...it's okay

GORDON
I don't know. Thank you for coming here.
I hope you like my furniture
I hope you enjoy my furniture
I think I'm falling in love with you

DEVON
Really?

GORDON
Sorry

DEVON
No it's

GORDON

I'm so amazed
I'm so amazed
You just talked for so long, with such force
And it caught me off guard
I don't even hear the construction anymore,
do you?

DEVON

No

GORDON

I guess that when days are significant
Like this one is
Everything gets a little quieter and stranger
And we can use our ability to talk to see what
comes out
Can I ask you a crazy question?

DEVON

Yes

GORDON

Do you like what I'm about

DEVON

I think I do yeah
You're really nice

GORDON

Can you take off your clothes?
You can say no but
Devon I
Sorry, I

Pause.

DEVON
Okay. Of course.
I said I would.

> Devon starts taking off his clothes.

All the way?

GORDON
What?

DEVON
All the way?

GORDON
No, that's okay.

> Pause. Gordon looks at Devon.

You're very beautiful.

DEVON
Thanks.

> Pause.

What are we, uh...
Are you

GORDON
Yes, okay

> Gordon takes off his shirt, slowly. Devon helps.

DEVON
Are you okay?

GORDON
Yes, I'm fine.

> Gordon finishes taking off his shirt.
> They stand there looking at each other.

I'm not mentally retarded.

DEVON
What. I didn't say you were.

GORDON
I know
I just
There was something about the way you

DEVON
Oh, I didn't...
That makes me sad. That you thought I was

GORDON
Oh, sorry.

> Pause.

I have Moebius syndrome, which is an
extremely rare craniofacial disorder. And I
have spinal problems. Meanwhile I'm an
extremely intelligent guy.

DEVON
You seem like an extremely intelligent guy.

GORDON
What are some of your favorite films?

DEVON
What?

GORDON
Are there films you like?

DEVON
Not really.

GORDON
Do you play any music?

DEVON
Ummm not since I was a kid. Actually, this is
funny because I was thinking about this just
like today or yesterday. So like when I was in
elementary school, I used to play in this
xylophone band.
It was like,
It was like,
So every year the music teacher was obsessed
with a different instrument and that year it
was the xylophone year. And so we'd play these
songs by George Orff? We made a CD.
I wonder where that is.

                    Pause.

Probably in that one basket at my aunt's.

                    Pause.

I don't know why I was in that band, but I
remember being really, really, really into this
music. I guess that was right after my mom
died so that makes sense. I remember just like
fucking destroying that xylophone. Like
fucking destroying that xylophone.

GORDON
Oh wow, Devon.
Fascinating
George Orff!
I think it's Carl.
Carl Orff.

                    Pause.

DEVON
I'm uh
I guess I just need to say that I'm becoming
uncomfortable.

GORDON
Why?

DEVON
I don't know. Cuz like

GORDON
Is it because of the way I look?

DEVON
No, I just, I got confused
I just don't know what we're doing here.

GORDON
Well, isn't it obvious?

DEVON
But we're just standing here.

                    Pause.

Are you okay?

Wheelchair

GORDON
Yes, why.

DEVON
You seem...

GORDON
I'm just tired.

DEVON
Yeah. What do you want to do with me?

GORDON
I want to
Hm
I don't know
I suddenly loved you
And I suddenly thought that
thought I should
have sex with you.

DEVON
Okay yeah, that's what I figured
And like, don't worry, cuz

                    Pause.

GORDON
Great.

                    Pause.

Do you mind if I take a nap?

DEVON
A nap?

GORDON
I suddenly got so tired
So tired and sad

DEVON
No, yeah, that's fine. Take a nap.

GORDON
Thanks. Sometimes I feel the whole world
And it makes me so tired that I need to
take a nap.
But that's okay, because my naps help the
world go round.

DEVON
I love naps. Totally.
Should I take the furniture and leave?

GORDON
Well no...
Can you just stay in the apartment?

DEVON
Stay in the apartment

GORDON
Just hang out in the apartment
Until I wake

DEVON
Okay yeah and

GORDON
Just if you

DEVON
Yeah okay

GORDON
It's just nice to have someone else here.
On my last day

DEVON
Yeah that's

GORDON
I feel as though this little place didn't get
enough love.

DEVON
Yeah.

GORDON
I don't want to move
But yes, I think I have to.
Because
Everything
Everything is changes
I mean everything changes
Everything is changes
Haha
You never get used to it!
Okay, just a little one then

> Gordon lies down on the mattress. Devon
> turns off the light and goes into the kitchen.
>
> He gets out his phone and texts. He looks
> around.
>
> There's a knock at the door. Devon looks
> towards the door. Stands up. Considers
> going to wake Gordon up.
>
> There's a knock at the door again. Devon
> retreats into the bathroom.

Now Sascha is here. She has a big bandage
on her cheek.

SASCHA
Hello?

She looks around.

Hello?

Devon comes out of the bathroom.

DEVON
Hi sorry. I'm
Sorry

SASCHA
Oh

DEVON
Sorry

SASCHA
Who are you?

DEVON
I'm Devon. Sorry I'm just

SASCHA
Is my uncle here?

DEVON
That man?

SASCHA
What?

DEVON
Like, the man who lives here?

SASCHA
Yes.

DEVON
He's your uncle?

SASCHA
Yeah. Uh
Where is he?

DEVON
He's taking a nap.

SASCHA
Oh.
Okay.

> She moves towards his bedroom.

DEVON
Um, he's really tired though.

SASCHA
Oh.
Well, it's important.

DEVON
Okay, he just got really tired and sad.
I think he's sad about moving?

SASCHA
He said he was moving?

DEVON
Yeah

SASCHA

That's good!

That's great!

Oh, great. Okay, okay, okay. Okay, this will be okay. Great. Also, sorry! You should leave.

DEVON

Why?

SASCHA

Because I still own this building and you're here illegally.

So is my uncle.

And that's not your fault!

It's just sometimes you have to wake up and be like—okay, I have to do this, I have to suck it up and do this, I have to confront that person, and I just have to get confront them and get it done, because that's just how it is, and I'm not evil, and he's, you know, he's struggling, but this is just the way things are and we have to move forward and I'll do everything I can to make it easier for everyone, but I'm not all-powerful you know?

DEVON

Yeah.

SASCHA

So

DEVON

Okay, but I just have to take this furniture. And I have to wait for my friend to pick me up. Well he's not really my friend, but he has a car

SASCHA

You're buying the furniture?

DEVON
No just, it's free
It's like
An internet
I

SASCHA
Well, go for it. I've got this company coming in
to start tearing shit down like now

DEVON
Yeah I know but

SASCHA
Yeah, just start taking it down
I'll just
I'm just gonna

>   She goes into Gordon's bedroom.
>   Devon lingers behind her.

SASCHA
Uncle Gordon?

>   Pause.

Uncle Gordon!

>   Gordon stirs awake. He looks at her.

GORDON
Hi, Sascha.

SASCHA
It's time to go. Why aren't you packed?
Why aren't you ready?

GORDON
Hi, Sascha. It's so good to see you.

SASCHA
Did you get my note?

GORDON
What note?

SASCHA
Oh wait no. I know you saw my note.
I know you saw my fucking note. It was
on a poster-board. You saw it.

> She sees the note under his mattress.
> It's on a poster-board. It's huge!

Oh my God! Look, here it is.

> She picks it up.

Read this to me.

GORDON
"UNCLE GORDON, THIS BUILDING IS BEING
TORN DOWN AND YOU HAVE TO LEAVE
BY DECEMBER 19. YOU CAN LIVE WITH
ME. I'M NOT TRYING TO BE MEAN. PLEASE
CALL ME. 718.789.7926. SASCHA."

> Pause.

I did see this.

SASCHA
So what's going on? Why are you sleeping?
The men are *downstairs*. They're here.

GORDON
I move slowly.

SASCHA
I know but you've had three months.

GORDON
Sascha please—I'm so tired.

SASCHA
I'm so sorry. I really am. I know things are hard
for you. But I don't live far away. You can sleep
later. I'm sorry.

GORDON
Sascha

SASCHA
You can sleep as long as you want. I have a
room for you.
A bed. It's extremely comfortable.

GORDON
I don't need a comfortable bed.
I just need a second

SASCHA
You've had so much time

GORDON
Okay but right now I just need

SASCHA
They're literally downstairs

GORDON
I just need to gather

SASCHA
Please, stand up. Can I help you?

GORDON
Just leave me alone for a second!
For one second!
You little
B-word

> Pause. Sascha leaves. Devon stares at Gordon.

Sorry, sorry, Devon.

DEVON
No that's okay.
I just
She wants me to leave
And I was wondering about the furniture
The timing of all that
Cuz my friend is

GORDON
Okay, okay, please, *please* just
Give me a moment
I had all these moments and suddenly
I have none

DEVON
Okay.

> Devon goes out to the kitchen. Sascha is there.
> She's crying.

Hey.

SASCHA
Hi. I'm sorry about all this.
He um

DEVON
No that's okay
I should go

SASCHA
Yeah, great

DEVON
I just really need to figure this out about
the furniture
I don't have any furniture in my

SASCHA
Of course.

DEVON
Yeah.

SASCHA
It's okay. I'm sorry.

DEVON
For what?

SASCHA
Nothing. Nothing.
He was my mom's brother and my mom died.
And like he didn't come to the funeral. This
was her building. She let him live here for free.
But this place should be burned to the ground.
So I sold it. I needed the money. I'm sorry
but I really needed the money. Why do I feel
bad about that? Anyway they're turning it
into artist studios.

DEVON
Oh cool.

SASCHA
And then I'm moving to Minneapolis.
And then, yeah, I'm moving to Minneapolis.

DEVON
Cool.

Gordon comes out.

GORDON
Here I come
Here I come slowly
Here I come slowly as you're kicking your own
uncle out—

SASCHA
Uncle Gordon!
You've had plenty of Oh my gosh.
You have no ground to Oh my gosh.
You lived here without paying any—
and you never thanked her!

GORDON
...it was complicated

SASCHA
You hated her for some reason

GORDON
You were both always treating me badly!

SASCHA
What?

GORDON
You were mean to me.

SASCHA
What are you talking about?

GORDON
You would hide behind her skirt when I came
to visit.

SASCHA
When? What
No I wouldn't...

GORDON
You would.
You were mean
You were scared of me

SASCHA
I tried to love you
You got mad at me when I came trick-or-
treating on Halloween.

GORDON
I hate Halloween. That goes way back. She
knew that.

SASCHA
It was my idea. I was six. I wasn't trying to
offend you.

GORDON
Other kids used to think I was wearing a *mask*.

SASCHA
You yelled at me.

GORDON
Okay okay I'm

SASCHA
And it wasn't just that. You were so
I grew up thinking you were a bad man

GORDON
No, don't call me that

SASCHA
You stole my mom's necklace, the one your
mom gave her
And you would pay men for sex and you
would buy them drugs
And you stole thousands of dollars from
my dad

GORDON
No I didn't

SASCHA
Yes you did!

GORDON
Okay okay! You are a very proud person and
you have a good memory.
I'm sorry
I'm sorry I was
I didn't mean to
I didn't mean to yell at you when you were six
You were scared
And I was scared

SASCHA
It's okay

GORDON
No, it was my fault
I got so angry at you
You were just a child

And I wanted to crush you
I wanted to crush you dead, just
For being scared of me.

Pause.

I'm sorry...

Pause.

SASCHA
And you didn't
You didn't come to see her

Pause.

GORDON
I'm sorry.

SASCHA
You didn't come to see her when she
was dying.

GORDON
What can I say? I'm sorry
I'm sorry
I'm broken
I'm sorry

Pause.

Sascha, listen.
I've discovered recently that um,
As though as a reward for all my suffering,
For all my sinning,
In that unfair way where those who sin the
most receive the most compassion,
I've been made lamed-vavnik.

SASCHA
What?

GORDON
I'm lamed-vavnik.

SASCHA
...What?

GORDON
I'm lamed-vavnik.

SASCHA
No you're not.

GORDON
...yes.

DEVON
Um hey Gordon? Gordon? Do you mind
If we just real quickly

GORDON
I am one of 36 special people in the world,
Sascha.
And were it not for us, all of us,
if even one of us was missing,
the world would come to an end.
It is my job to greet the Shekhinah.
It is my job to stay concealed.
I have mystic powers.
I often save the world!
Sometimes just by praying
Sometimes just by going to the bathroom
Sometimes just by listening to Barbra
Sometimes just by napping.

I'm telling you this because I think
I think you should know.

SASCHA
Uncle Gordon. If someone claims to be a
lamed-vavnik, that's proof that they're not one.

GORDON
Well, you're the only person I've told. I think
that's okay. I'm trying to explain. I'm trying to
atone. Come here.

> She takes a few steps towards him.

Come closer.

> He puts his hand on her head.

I forgive you.

SASCHA
You're not lamed-vavnik!

> She moves away from him.

DEVON
Hey can I

SASCHA
Oh yes, sorry
What's your name?

DEVON
Devon.

SASCHA
Gordon, what are we doing with Devon?

GORDON
I don't know. I don't have any idea what to do
with Devon
I look at him and I feel shame

DEVON
What?

SASCHA
Oh my God. Who is he? What did he do
for you?

GORDON
He's beautiful
We might be in love

DEVON
Oh well actually this was all through
Craigslist...

SASCHA
Why is he here?

GORDON
Well. I've never had sex in this apartment.
I wanted to have sex before I went away.

DEVON
I

SASCHA
Okay. So. Have you done it yet?

GORDON
No, I got tired.

SASCHA
Well, I'm not gonna wait around for you to
do it.

DEVON
Look, we didn't discuss that before I came
I just thought
We had some nice conversations—
some nice words
No, things got weird for a second or like
Then I talked for a long time, which was weird
And then we thought
I think we both thought there was a
connection
I went crazy for a second
I mean it was nice
Can I just
I'll take whatever.
And actually hm
Maybe I'll just go.

SASCHA
No, here, here's
Devon—can you wait outside?
And then come back in when we're gone?
To get the stuff?
Is that fair?

DEVON
That's actually perfect
I'll go to the
I'll wait at the

SASCHA
Great.
Fuck.

DEVON
Okay
Thanks
So
Thanks
Okay
I guess I'll

SASCHA
Yeah

DEVON
Bye Gordon
Um, I'm sorry we didn't get to know each other
better, or
I'm sorry for my monologue

GORDON
That's okay
I hope you do well, Devon

DEVON
Thanks, you too.

GORDON
Thanks

DEVON
Um, I believe you
That you're lamed-vavnik.

GORDON
Oh, thank you.

DEVON
And and
And you can email me at that email
Just, whenever you want

Just email me whenever you want to get erotic
Cuz I like doing it, it's something I like doing
And I will for you anytime okay? Okay.
Bye

Devon leaves.

SASCHA
What do you need me to do to get you out
of here?

GORDON
Nothing, I'm ready.

SASCHA
You're not taking anything?

GORDON
I found it all on the street
It will end up where it needs to be
With Devon
Or
Somewhere else

SASCHA
What about your record player? You found that
on the street?

GORDON
Oh I bought that on Target.com. It's great.
Just leave it.
I don't need anything.
I'm too holy now.
All of these things—they were good to me.
Thank you things, thank you for being
good to me.

SASCHA
Great. Great. Thank you. I love you.

GORDON
I'm angry at you!

SASCHA
What

GORDON
Couldn't you have kept this one unlisted?
Huh, Sascha? Couldn't you have kept
it unlisted? Did you need to sell every
single unit?

SASCHA
Yes I had to, I had to! I don't want to manage
anything I just needed to sell this
My non-profit folded
I had to
And I am opening my home to you. I barely
even know you and I'm opening my

GORDON
That's nice that's nice

SASCHA
Yeah it's nice

GORDON
Do you have a cat?

SASCHA
Yes.

GORDON
I'm allergic to cats.

SASCHA
Jesus Christ.
We'll figure...fuck. Is it bad

GORDON
Yes

SASCHA
Oh God...
Well I can't get rid of...Oh God, Agnes
We'll figure something out

GORDON
Everything is hollow
We are not real
Going out there—I will dissolve
I can't fuse with the world
I just want things to stay the way they were.

SASCHA
Uncle Gordon. Uncle Gordon. You're going to
be okay. Listen to me. Are you listening? You
will be okay. We will love each other. We have
to leave here. It's not even a conversation.
We have to leave here. Change is good. Change
is productive—

GORDON
Yeah yeah.
Sascha I can't help it. I've been meaning to
ask you:
What is that on your face?

SASCHA
It's a
What?
It's a bandage cuz I
I had a pimple. I had a really big pimple.

Can we not talk about this? I just had a really
big pimple.

GORDON
Okay.

SASCHA
I'm sorry. Fuck.
Look, I just had a really big pimple.
Okay. Okay. Okay.
I was sitting in my apartment. It was after my
mom's funeral. And I felt this thing rise up
on my cheek—like that under-pain, like that
throbbing under-thing? I knew a pimple was
coming, I knew it was big. The next day it
showed up. It was the size of a quarter. It had
four whiteheads. And it kept growing. It took
over my face. By the end it had ten whiteheads,
I'm not even kidding. It hurt so much I wanted
to die. But I had so much to do. My non-profit
was folding and I had to write 600 emails.
I was sitting at my desk in my apartment and
my pimple started to talk to me. I heard it in
ten simultaneous devil voices. It said: "the
worst thing in the world is doing anything at
all." It told me to hate myself, and so I did.
It told me to hate everything and everyone,
and so I did. I listened to that fucking pimple.
The pimple told me that I was going to kill
myself one day, and I believed it. I thought
I was the biggest piece of shit, I thought I was
evil. I wanted to do the will of the pimple.
It was the only thing that got me out of bed.
I obeyed the pimple. I don't want to hurt anyone. I want to make the world a better place.
But I hate everyone and I hate everything.
Hate is my great gift. Hate is the only thing I
have access to right now. I was lying on my

bathroom floor, wanting to die, and my pimple
told me that out there is overpopulated with
The Clean. The pimple hates how clean it's
getting. I hate it too. The pimple told me to get
out of here, to sell everything, to take you with
me, somewhere far away, and try to be simple
and messy. I don't know how long it's been
since you were really out there but there is
more going wrong than you might suspect. The
world's not on fire but people are cracking open
in ridiculous embarrassing ways. I hate this,
Uncle Gordon. I hate being here. I hate doing
this. I'm sorry. I'm sorry if you can tell how
much I hate you, and myself. I don't think hate
means not helping. I remembered you.
I remembered that there was something good
about you. I see and I remember and it makes
me sad. I never expected to hear myself
glitching like this. I understand now that the
greatest love affair of my life has been with my
own decay. I'm passionately in love with
my own rotting. That was a stupid thing to say.
Anyway eventually I got a fork and I started
piercing my pimple with the fork. I started
stabbing at it slowly and then hard and it oozed
and broke. And I heard the pimple's screams as
it died, and as it was dying, it pointed out
everything I'd ever done in my life that was
shitty and petty and selfish and deceitful. It
knew about how I'd squeeze my cat so hard and
wished it would die. It knew about all those
times I'd emotionally cheated on my big
boyfriend. It knew how sometimes I would
watch myself grieving and wonder whether
my grief was beautiful and marketable and
cool. It also told me how and when I would die,
and then the pimple died. But the hole won't
stop bleeding on my face. So now I have to

keep this bandage on my face. And now almost
everything I say these days is heavy with
the weight of my death, I have that wisdom
about me, isn't that cool. Oh, fuck, anyway,
it's important to surrender and we are given
ourselves by God, how wonderful, how
wonderful. It's getting. And then I think,
I really do think that someone hit me on the
back of the head. I could hardly understand
them. Did you see the way they looked at me?
I have these horrible nightmares—those
shuttles in the sky, getting higher and higher,
falling off the tracks and plummeting down.
But I realized recently, I remembered from the
dream that there's always all this time before
the shuttle goes off the tracks—this time when
people are just looking at me. All of these
beautiful young people across the car. The
edges of their eyes, twitching. Someone looks
away. Someone doesn't. No one sits next
to me. And then I hear someone say "this is
the street where it lives" which is what I heard
one day when I was five, playing in my yard.
It. It. This is the street where *it* lives. And I ran
into my house and my father was weeping
and praying, with his tefillin, phylacteries
spooling out of his head, and he shouted at me.

GORDON
No, Sascha, that's my memory.

SASCHA
No, I remember this. The Orthodox community
in Monsey. Myself as a little boy. Growing up,
drifting away from everyone. And so the
shuttle plummeting in my nightmare—that's
a gift I give myself, to get out of that train.
To fuse with all of them. All of our faces melt.

And I try to help. And these kids, Agnes! These
kids need us! Meanwhile I don't feel human.
Oh fuck this fuck this fuck this seriously fuck
this. When will I be the kind of person I want
to be? What kind of person do I want to be?
I can barely think. I haven't read anything. I
never know what people are talking about.
I'm lazy. I'm afraid of talking on the phone. I'm
a quilt of mistakes. I've been coughing for
2 straight weeks. "I, I, I." What a jerk. Fuck you.
Fuck you, I hate you. I'm sorry. I'm interested
in living spaces. It's always living in spaces.
I got a haircut. I got a little thing of whiskey. I
felt my flub as I lonelied through Soho. Aware
of my aware. Construction sites are. Get it
done—move on. Don't be afraid. Try to be true.
Do not exploit. I have not done anything that
terrifies me enough. Everybody files into
separate architectures. Why do we go places?
Why do we sit down? What does it mean to
be terrified *enough?* How are we supposed
to know what's going to happen? Why does
talking matter at all? Why can't I touch
everyone? Why do I have to be here right now
doing this? How will I do the thing that feels
the way I want to feel? How do I want to feel?
Unmoored. Like someone with no identity.
Like invisible water spooling into people's
brains. Getting inside. Hating everyone and
knowing *exactly why.* Get me out of here. Have
you noticed how everyone talks all the time
about the present moment? Let us live in the
past. Let us dread without cease. Ummm.

Pause.

GORDON
Okay. Well. I love you.

He looks around one more time.

This is such a significant day.

Pause.

I think I'll have more to say once we get more
used to each other.
Or once I've taken a bath.
Or an uninterrupted nap.
This room has too much of my righteousness
in it.
It was getting stuffy with my righteousness,
and everything started breaking.
I don't know
I don't know how to make this feel better
I don't know why I'm alive
I don't know if this is really happening
When I'm by myself, I feel holy and watched
When I'm with other people, I start to feel evil
I start to fuck up
I don't want to fuck up, Sascha
I'll go wherever I'm supposed to go
And I'll try to be good
Whatever,
Whatever, it's fine.
Maybe before I die, I'll make a difference in one
person's life. On purpose.
Instead of everybody's life on accident.
I'm talking about you.
Maybe we'll be friends.
Maybe we'll lonely together.
And then I'll email Devon for my important
sex thoughts
But then maybe I'll meet someone real
Who I'll let touch me
And maybe I'll feel real
I don't know. My brain's all fuzzy.

Wheelchair

God is telling me to, um
God is telling me to, um
Let's go.

They leave. The room is quiet.

Then, the volume on a conversation slowly
rises. Somehow, we know that this
conversation was under all the conversations
above. And somehow we know that it is
the card table who is talking.

CARD TABLE
I don't know, I
It's not that I
Wanted to feel that way
It's just that I couldn't help it
I mean
Truly truly I could not help it
I was so attracted to this uhhh
I mean honestly I don't know how old
This little
Boy
Was
And it's ah again guys it wasn't a sexual thing
it was
It was a uhhh
You know j—
that feeling that you get in between your legs
where it's
Uhh
I guess uhh
I guess it is a little bit sexual but it's more it's
uh it's cosmic it's uh it's like uh it's it's it's it's
like you feel something that was meant uhhh
To be and it's
It's not coming out right
What I'm saying is that he was walking he was

walking through the store with his parents
and I think there were some other siblings
around and it was the way that he was looking
at me umm the way that he was looking at
everything?
And it was just like this understanding, this
knowledge
And you know I
I wanted so bad to
I wanted him
You know I wanted him in my life I guess
that's that's really what it was
I wanted him I wanted this boy you know in
my life
And you know okay that so the *feeling*
There was the *feeling*
And the feeling definitely did feel if I'm being
honest
Okay yes it did feel
Like
A little bit uhhh you know
Sexy and that that ummm
Ahh
Fact is I wanted him to crawl on me you know
It was like it felt RIGHT
And umm it didn't feel wrong in the moment
and it was only later when I you know learned
more you know about what's you know when
it comes to being attracted to people uh it's
better to go with the older ones and ummm
and I have I do I am for real, and it was just this
one and it was like oh there was that one time
with the little boy, that felt real, and I don't
know I think what I'm saying is that I believe
in souls and I like you know there wasn't what
am I gonna I wasn't gonna do anything to this
kid you know it was like a soul thing you know
it was like oh man this could really work out

I was hoping you know I was hoping in that
moment that it WOULD work out.
And uhhh
and then of course
it didn't
and then

CHAIR
Yeah

CARD TABLE
...you know

CHAIR
Right

CARD TABLE
...there was a feeling of loss there

FAN
Yeah

Pause.

CARD TABLE
...you know that's that's that's that's really all
I'm saying that's you know there's not uh that
I'm not trying to like trying to like make some
like big case for like you know for like you
know like table-child love you know it's not
that it was just like this one time. I shouldn't
have even mentioned it I'm sorry.

CHAIR
No no no it's fine it's fine, table, it's, honestly
it's fine

Card Table sighs. Pause.

CARD TABLE
...even this pause right now is like freaking
me out
Like you guys are all, like you're all just
Both of you are judging me

FAN
I'm
I'm
I'm definitely judging you but I'm, I'm getting
a little bit closer to seeing what you are
talking about.

CARD TABLE
Okay great, I mean honestly like who uh can
we just like forget that I ever even uhh chimed
in to your fucking conversation.
It's just that you said that thing
You said that thing about loss and I
Uhhh fan you should keep telling your story.
I'm sorry.

FAN
No, no, I'm uhh...yeah, so.

Fan starts oscillating.

So, yeah I was just
SO I was just um, asking, like did I tell you
about the hot springs?
When I was in a hot springs? Uh, at the
hot springs?
People would get too hot when they were,
uh...when they were in the hot springs...
Sometimes the people would over-heat?
So they ran a couple cords from the office,
and I was, I was out there. Just in case.

And I saw this old guy push a wheelchair over,
and it was him and his wife, I think. He pushed
his wife over. He didn't *push* her *over*...
not like that.
No, he just, he was pushing her, wheeling her,
towards the, she was in a wheelchair.
She was...um. She was like, bent. Like bent up.
She was disabled. She...
She had a disability.
And they were both in their underwear.
And.
And.
They were both in their underwear and—

CHAIR
No!

FAN
What?

CHAIR
No you haven't told me about this.

CARD TABLE
Me neither.

FAN
Oh.
Great. Perfect. Better. Good. Okay so.

CHAIR
I was waiting to hear a part that I knew, if I
knew it, but I don't remember this story,
I would have remembered it if I remembered it.

FAN
Right.

CHAIR
Sorry.

FAN
No, right. Okay, right, good.
Ah, anyway.
Ah man.
I don't know.

CHAIR
What?

FAN
Nothing.

CHAIR
No, what?

FAN
Nothing. I feel stuck.

CHAIR
You're not. You're going. You're going.

FAN
But it's what I feel.

CHAIR
I'm sorry.

FAN
No, it's...

CHAIR
What?

FAN
Nothing. Anyway.

CHAIR
No—

FAN
Anyway anyway anyway.

CHAIR
No what? Is this about how you think you're
broken? Because you're not.

FAN
Okay.

CHAIR
You're not broken. I am. You so clearly work,
and I'm so clearly broken. Remember?

FAN
No you're not, chair.

CHAIR
Yes. I am. I don't work. I never work.
I'm lazy and broken. I'm not right.
Nobody cares about me or needs me.
I waste all my time feeling sorry for myself.
I give away all my power.
And I'm sick. I'm sick.
I'm really sick.

> Oscillation stops. Pause. Oscillation starts.

FAN
Can we not—can we not talk about that?

CARD TABLE
Yeah.

CHAIR
Okay.

FAN
Sorry.

CHAIR
No I'm sorry.

CARD TABLE
I'm not sorry.

CHAIR
Okay well I am sorry.

CARD TABLE
I *know* I was just
Ugh nevermind I'm just
I'm not gonna talk.

FAN
It's fine. Anyway.
I was at the hot springs.
The old man stopped the wheelchair. Stopped
pushing his old wife.
And he slid off his underwear. And his big
wrinkled penis plopped out.
And then he took off her bra.
And then he slid down her underwear.
And they were both naked, and their bodies
were so old. I didn't mind.
And then he pulled her up, like, hoisted.
Her up.
And like um.
He walked her down into the water, into the
hot springs.
And she was smiling.

And she smiled so big when the water got up to
her waist, like reacted so big, immediately.
And he settled her in. Into the hot springs.
And then he settled in.
And then they were sitting there.
And he reached over and scratched her head.
He scratched her hair. For a long time.
And she smiled again.
And then suddenly he was, uh...
He was rubbing her breasts. He was rubbing
her breasts.
In front of me.
They never looked at me. But they knew
I was there.
He rubbed her breasts. For a long time.
And she smiled and closed her eyes.
It was really nice.
And later, much later...he hoisted her out of the
springs, and back into the wheelchair.
And he picked up their underwear and handed
it to her...well. I mean he put the underwear
on her lap. And then he wheeled her away. And
they were both still naked.
And I watched them go away. And it was one
of my favorite nights ever.
That was a while ago.
I was a little bit different then.
I was kind of different.
Like my whole personality was different. Haha.

       Oscillation stops. Pause. Starts.

CHAIR
You've lived so much more.
And you're so much more interesting.

       Card Table sighs.

I don't have the courage to do anything.
I'm just going to rot.

FAN
I'm sure that's not true.

CHAIR
It is.

FAN
I'm sure there are some cool things about you.

CHAIR
There aren't.
Well.
Well.
I don't know if you consider this cool,
but I can speak Russian.

FAN
That is cool. That is definitely cool.
Show me.

CHAIR
Nah, later. I have too many problems right now.

FAN
No you don't.

CHAIR
Yes I do.

FAN
Like what?

CHAIR
A horrible pain rippling through me.
Like I'm rotting.

I'm exhausted all the time.
I feel so sick.
And no one believes me. Like you. You don't
believe me.

FAN
Okay. Well.
You're right. I don't believe you.
But.
Suffering is suffering.
But.
I don't know. At any given...
At any given moment, in the world, rooms are
getting blown to bits.
Rooms and everything in them.
Blown to bits.

CHAIR
I don't follow.

FAN
We're here, all alone.

CHAIR
Right. Wait. What?

CARD TABLE
Yeah, what?

FAN
I think we just got left. I think that's what
happened.

CARD TABLE
Wait, what?
He's coming back, right?

CHAIR
Yeah, he is. That's what he does.

FAN
We might have been forgotten about. We might
have a lot more time ahead of us.

CHAIR
Wait what.

FAN
Anyway I don't want to argue about it. All I'm
saying is that we *could* be abandoned. At any
time. We could. That's kind of scary. But at least
we're not getting blown to bits.
At least we're not a part of the problem.
The problems.
Out there.

CHAIR
Maybe we are and we just don't know it. We
don't know what this room could be doing to
the equation, you know? The room and us in it,
what we could be doing, to make things worse.
It's possible. It's possible that we're complicit.
It's possible that we're evil. Or that we're being
used for evil, and we just don't know it.
We definitely don't have good in our lives.
We definitely don't have any good in our lives.
We don't have anyone taking off our underwear
and lowering us into the hot springs.
We don't have anyone scratching our heads.
We don't have anyone rubbing our breasts.
We don't have someone who cares for us,
slowly, one by one, with big old hands, so that
we smile.

FAN
Well, fuck.
Fuck. That's not why I told that story.
I didn't tell you that story to feed you more
shit.
Into your shit.
The way you make everything into your shit.
I told you that to tell you my thing, my thing
that I was holding onto.
This thing that I liked.
I didn't want to think about how I can't be the
old people.
I just liked being there to see them.
They had their good thing and it made me
think about my good things.
And I just wanted to tell you.
Fuck.
Fuck.
Fuck, chair.
Fuck you.

Oscillation stops. Pause.

CHAIR
Sorry.
Sorry.
Fan?
Sorry.
Sorry.
I just need to be grateful. I need to be more
grateful.
Fuck.

Chair starts speaking in broken Russian.

Спасибо за все NAILS, спасибо за все SLABS OF
WOOD, спасибо за GLASS, спасибо за все

PATCHES OF DIRT, спасибо за весь бетон, за горшки для мешания, ткань, клей, песок, груз. Мы просто стараемся делать хорошую работу. Мы просто стараемся помочь. Мы ничего не значим. Мы ничего не будем значить. Возможно мы будем что-то значить. Для всех, кто SUFFERING и обременен, это нормально быть ANGRY ABOUT IT. Посмотрите на себя со стороны и попробуйте отнестись к себе, как кому-то, кого Вы нежно любите. В этом нет ничего страшного, стыдного или эгоистичного. Вы бесконечно любимы. Любите Бога, любите себя, любите тех, кто Вас окружает. LET YOURSELF BE SAD, существовать в этом состоянии и потом FEAST ON YOUR CRAZY и прекрасной жизни.

>   Pause.

I wish I were a wheelchair.

>   Oscillation starts.

FAN
Well, you're not.

CARD TABLE
Yeah, you're not.

>   Long pause.

CHAIR
Hey, card table?

CARD TABLE
What

CHAIR
We're just furniture.
Isn't that dumb?

CARD TABLE
No! Furniture is so important!

CHAIR
...okay
...but sometimes I wonder if we've been created
for total pointless evil?

CARD TABLE
NO.

CHAIR
Oh.

CARD TABLE
I mean it!

CHAIR
Okay

CARD TABLE
Damnit dude
FURNITURE IS SO IMPORTANT.
AND GOOD.

FAN
And appliances.

CARD TABLE
AND APPLIANCES.

CHAIR
OKAY OKAY

CARD TABLE
Fuck, chair
Fuck

CHAIR
What

CARD TABLE
Just like—fucking calm down
We are important
We are awesome
Fuck

>Suddenly, Devon comes in and starts taking the stuff from the apartment. He folds up the card table and starts piling stuff on top of that.
>
>He deflates the air mattress and takes that too. He takes some stuff off-stage.

CHAIR
What's going on?

FAN
I don't know.

>Devon comes back.
>
>He unplugs the fan. He approaches the record player.
>
>The record player suddenly turns on.
>
>It's elementary-school kids playing Carl Orff on xylophones.
>
>Devon can't believe it. He listens. He laughs.

Then he unplugs the record player, takes that and the fan. He looks at the chair, and decides not to take it. And he leaves.

Silence. Chair is there. Fridge is there. The stage is so much more empty.

CHAIR
Um
Hello?

Hello?

Hello?

Hello...?

Oh hello?

Hello?

The power suddenly surges back on. Fridge gasps.

FRIDGE (singing Barbra)
Where is the wonder that I once felt?
Watching snowflakes melt as a child.
Where is the wonder that I once knew?
When the sky of blue turned wild?

CHAIR
Fridge?
Is that you?

FRIDGE
What happened? Was I singing?

CHAIR
Yeah you were singing.

FRIDGE
Oh wow, I was singing.

CHAIR
Are you okay?

FRIDGE
I thought I was dead.

CHAIR
Oh yeah, I thought you were too.

FRIDGE
Oh my God.

CHAIR
Are you okay?

FRIDGE
Yeah I mean
I was singing
How did I sound?

CHAIR
You sounded pretty good

FRIDGE
Wow

CHAIR
Yeah.
But you're okay?

FRIDGE
I'm okay

CHAIR
Wow
We all thought you were dead

FRIDGE
I thought I was dead too
But now I know that I was having a really
dumb dream

CHAIR
What was it?

FRIDGE
I was on the battlefield
I was under a corpse on the big battlefield
It was the end of everything
Someone uh
Someone found me, yeah
And there were some snacks in me
So they ate the snacks and survived

CHAIR
That's awesome

FRIDGE
I don't know. Kinda dumb.

Pause.

Where is everyone?

CHAIR
I don't know, they got took

FRIDGE
Damn

CHAIR
But it's okay I think he'll be right back...

FRIDGE
Okay.
Damn.
Oof.
Okay.

Pause.

We'll be okay.
Let's talk about something.

CHAIR
Okay.

Pause.

Have I uh
Have I ever told you? I want to be a wheelchair.

FRIDGE
Oh yeah? Why?

CHAIR
Well because of the
You know the…
Think about it.

FRIDGE
No tell me, just tell me.

Pause.

CHAIR
A wheelchair is needed.

Pause.

FRIDGE
…Oh yeah?

CHAIR
Yeah and they see the world. And they dance.
And they're needed.

FRIDGE
A chair is needed too.

CHAIR
Yeah some of them.
But I'm not.
I'm just not.
I'm just a non-being.

FRIDGE
No
Oh man
No
It's funny I

CHAIR
What

FRIDGE
I don't know
I just, I guess I
Yeah, it's sad.
I can tell you're uh...
Yeah. I've been there.
But then I woke from the dead.
And I was singing.
Didn't know that was gonna happen.
And I think I smell okay too.
And uh

               Pause.

Yeah.
For so long, for me, it was *can you, can you*?
In all things, can you *can you*
And I don't know if can.
And I don't know if I'm needed.
But I know that I *need*, or...
That I
Uh

               Pause.

I think what I think is that uh
...
There is no non-being.

               Pause.

CHAIR
Yeah, I like that optimism.
I like that optimism.
Coming from you, it feels earned.

They are there. They are there! The sound of footsteps. Shouts. Construction rising in pitch. A loud drill. A saw. Something falling. Closer and closer, right on top of us. Oh no! The end.

CHAIR's Russian prayer translation:
Thank you to all the nails, thank you to all the
slabs of wood, thank you to all the glass,
thank you to all the patches of dirt, thank you
to all the concrete, the mixing pots, the fabric,
the glue, the sand, the weight. Thank you
for all the hands that put us together. We're
just trying to do a good job. We're just trying
to help. We don't matter. We won't matter.
We might matter. For all who are suffering and
burdened, it is okay to be angry about it. Step
outside yourself and treat yourself as someone
who you love dearly. There's nothing wrong
with this, nothing shameful or selfish about it.
You are infinitely loved. Love God, love yourself,
love everyone around you. Let yourself be sad,
exist in that place, and then feast on your crazy
and lovely life.

Portions of this prayer were written
by my sister, Monica Arbery.

AFTERWORD

I'm barely able to think of *Wheelchair* as a manuscript. I think of
it as a night. A night and some days. Or a cycle of gift-giving.
A string of recalibrations, slower and more honest than a normal
process. I think of it as December 19, 2016 at Dixon Place, and
there's Kimie taping out the set despite a bad cold. Daniel and I
go to buy her whiskey. Rachel's running lines with Kate in the
hallway. Sam's assembling the sound cues at the last minute.
Paris is running late from dog-walking, oh no. Dan and Mara and
Jack are making each other laugh behind the curtain. Jacob
and I are nervous. Matthew says he's not nervous at all, so now
I'm not either. Yes I am. We've got Leonard Cohen playing on the
record player on stage. My friends are in the audience, which
always astounds me. The show happens, slow and weird. At one
point, scripts in hand, Matthew and Paris lose their place. Later
we realize it was because they had different versions of the
script, since we'd printed Matthew's in bigger font. A light cue
gets skipped, so things get dark all at once, rather than slowly.
(Bill Callahan: *I used to be darker, then I got lighter, then I got dark
again.*) Because the chair was slightly misplaced, the audience
thinks Lamp is talking instead of Chair. But all the mistakes
seem purposeful. Or at least like there's room for them. There's
no failing here. Afterwards, Matthew's friend and collaborator
Ping Chong congratulates me and I thank him for leading me to
Matthew. Later Matthew tells me Ping actually thought the show
was a bit too long. Whatever, I agree. Now here's Jacob waiting
with Matthew for a cab in the cold. Jacob's vigilant heart. All
these vigilant hearts. We drink and strike set. I forget the card
table on the street, damn it. At two in the morning I lug my
roommate's mini-fridge back up the narrow stairs. I wake up
my roommate. He didn't know I had taken it and he's annoyed
and I'm sorry. I don't sleep. Three hours later I'm on a flight to
Wyoming for Christmas. My parents pick me up. We talk about
the play for five minutes and then I get quiet and foggy. Outside
it's snowing and flat gorgeous and we have a three-hour drive
ahead and I start the new remembering.

ACKNOWLEDGMENTS

Thank you Sofya Levitsky-Weitz. Thank you Kate Dakota Kremer and the word *evacuation*. Thank you Sam Barickman and Di Glazer. Thank you RJ Tolan and Graeme Gillis, and everyone in Youngblood. Thank you Dixon Place. Thank you Michael Bulger and Clubbed Thumb. Thank you Martha Beggerly. Thank you Kimie Nishikawa and Daniel Prosky. Thank you Drew Lewis and Kenny Polyak and Michael Yates Crowley and my small black Blizzard fan. Thank you Lilleth Gilmcher. Thank you Gregg Mozgala. Thank you Maia Safani. Thank you Liz Engelman and Tofte Lake Center. Thank you to the barn that was about to be torn down, for letting me walk through your wet rottingness and speak aloud large portions of this play. Thank you Monica and Julia Arbery. Thank you Yasunari Kawabata, for your palm-of-the-hand stories. Thank you Young Jean Lee. Thank you Rachel Sachnoff, Alexander Paris, Dan Giles, Mara Nelson-Greenberg, Jack Plowe. Thank you Matthew Joffe. Thank you Jacob Brandt. Thank you Rachel Kauder Nalebuff and Tessa Lee, for letting me hold this in my hands and thank you again.

WILL ARBERY is a playwright + performer + filmmaker from Texas + Wyoming. His play *PLANO* premiered at Clubbed Thumb's Summerworks in June 2018. He's currently under commission from Playwrights Horizons. His plays have been developed at Clubbed Thumb, Playwrights Horizons, Ojai Playwrights Conference, New Neighborhood, The New Group, EST/Youngblood, The Bushwick Starr, Alliance/Kendeda, White Heron, 100w Corsicana, Two Headed Rep, and Tofte Lake Center. He's a member of SPACE on Ryder Farm's Working Farm, EST's Youngblood, Calliope Theatre, and a former member of Clubbed Thumb's Early Career Writers Group. His dance work (with Kora Radella & Matty Davis) has been seen at Pioneer Works, The Watermill Center, and MCA Chicago. MFA: Northwestern University. BA: Kenyon College. He grew up the only boy among seven sisters. willarbery.com

3 Hole Press titles:

IS GOD IS—Aleshea Harris, 2017
BRIEF CHRONICLE, BOOKS 6-8—Alexander Borinsky, 2017
WHEELCHAIR—Will Arbery, 2018
THE IMMEASURABLE WANT OF LIGHT—Daaimah Mubashshir, 2018

For more information about **3 Hole Press**, visit 3holepress.org